100 Write-and-Learn
Sight Word
Practice Pages

Engaging Reproducible Activity Pages That Help Kids Recognize, Write, and Really LEARN the Top 100 High-Frequency Words That Are Key to Reading Success

SCHOLASTIC
PROFESSIONAL BOOKS

New York • Toronto • London • Auckland • Sydney • New Delhi
Mexico City • Hong Kong • Buenos Aires

P9-CQL-655

Scholastic Inc. grants teachers permission to photocopy the activity sheets for classroom use. No other part of this publication may be reproduced in whole or in part, or stored in a retrieval system, or transmitted in any form or by any means, electronic, mechanical, photocopying, recording, or otherwise, without written permission of the publisher. For information regarding permission, write to Scholastic Inc., 557 Broadway, New York, NY 10012.

Cover and interior design by Norma Ortiz
Illustrations by Jane Dippold

ISBN: 0-439-36562-7

Copyright © 2002 by Scholastic Inc. All rights reserved.

Contents

What are Sight Words?

Sight words, or high-frequency words, are the words most commonly encountered in any text. Often, these words do not follow regular rules of spelling, so children will not be able to easily decode the word—they must simply "know it when they see it." For instance, the word "the" appears about every tenth word in children's books!

There are approximately 600,000 words in the English language, but only 13 of them (*a, and, for, he, is, in, it, of, that, the, to, was, you*) account for more than 25% of the words in print! (Johns 1980). Children see such words all around them every day. They see them on the walls of their classroom, on signs and advertisements, and on all other types of environmental print. Some children "internalize" these words on their own after repeated exposure, while others will need more explicit instruction.

These practice sheets give children in-depth, hands-on experience with the top 100 sight words. When emergent readers can automatically recognize these words without having to stop to decode them letter by letter, their reading becomes more fluent—and their confidence soars! When they're comfortable with enough sight words, children will also free up lots of mental energy for higher-level thinking. They can focus their attention on making meaning from what they're reading, rather than on sounding out individual words.

You can use these pages in for whole-group, small-group, or individual work. However you choose to do so, mastering sight words builds a strong foundation for reading success!

The Dolch Word List

There are several widely recognized lists of high-frequency words—the Dolch Word List and the Frye Instant Word" list are among them. The words in this book are found on the Dolch Word List, though there is much overlap between lists. The words on this list account for more than 50% of the words found in textbooks today! However, both lists provide a core of words that need to be developed at a high-speed recognition level.

A Note to the Teacher: As you glance through this book, you'll notice that many high-frequency words carry little meaning and are not necessarily as easy to define as nouns. They are known as "function words," rather than "content words." Though they may appear to not carry a clear meaning, they have a strong impact on the flow and coherence of any text we read.

Using These Pages

Each practice page follows the same format and children complete each page the same way. They:

- trace the word along guiding gray lines several times as they say it aloud (so that they have an auditory experience as well as a visual one). A picture near the practice lines illustrates the use of the word. Children might begin by writing the word in the air.

- write the word themselves.

- cut out the letter cards along the dotted lines at the bottom of the page, mix them up, and then put the letters in the proper order. This gives them hands-on experience with each letter and helps them observe each letter's position in the word. They might also turn them over, move them around and then challenge themselves to reassemble in the right order once they are turned rightside-up. (For an extra challenge, try mixing up words from several worksheets!)

- paste their letter cards in the right boxes in the sentence, then write the same letters in the same sentence.

- finish by writing their own sentence using the word.

Sight Word Activities

At the end of this book you'll find reproducible pages that can be used for practice:

◉ Search for the Sight Words (page 109-110)
Children search for the sight words on the list and circle them. You can also make your own word searches with any sight words you wish using graph paper.

◉ Sight Word Stationery (page 111)
Reproducible stationery for any writing activity!

◎**Sight Word Bingo** (page 112)

Have children randomly write a sight word (list 25-30 on the board) in each square. Then, call out words one at a time. Have children put a marker or mark on the square with that word. The first child to get five across calls "bingo!" Speed up for a challenge! Children might also enjoy leading this game.

Try these other sight words games and activities:

◎**Silly Sentences**

You'll need a stack of index cards and markers in different colors. Using different colors for each word group, write words or phrases on index cards: articles (*a*, *an*, *the*, *these*, *this, that, those*), pronouns (*he, she, him, her, you, I, me, they*) adjectives (*big, good, bad,* and so on), nouns (*boy, girl, dinosaur, man,* and so on), verbs (*went, goes, is, will,* and so on), and prepositional phrases (*to the store, in the house, with his friend,* and so on). Using a pocket chart, children manipulate and arrange the cards to form silly sentences and read them aloud. Children can create their own cards as they need them to complete their sentences.

◎**Hangman**

Choose a simple sentence that includes several sight words, such as:
  • Do you like this game?
  • There is a ladybug in my hair!
  • The cat was big and striped.
Play hangman with the group (children guess letters and you write them in the blanks).

◎**Words Within Words**

Choose any piece of text (you can photocopy a page from a book, use children's own writing, or your own writing on chart paper from a previous activity such as morning message). Give children highlighters and have them search for and highlight "words within words"—small sight words that can be found "hiding" in bigger words. For instance, in the word favorite, *or* and *it* are "hiding."

◎**Concentration**

On a set of index cards, write each sight word twice (one per card). Children turn all the cards facedown and turn over two at a time, trying to make a match. If they do so, they keep the cards and take another turn; if they do not, they turn the cards back over and the next player has a turn.

a

Trace the word and say it aloud:

a a a a a a

I have a new hat.

Write the word:

Cut out the letter at the bottom of the page. Then paste it in the square to finish the sentence:

I have ☐ new hat.

Write the word to finish the sentence:

I have ___ new hat.

Write your own sentence using the word:

a

and

Name: _____

Trace the word and say it aloud:

and and and

cookies **and** milk

Write the word:

_____

- - - - - - - - - - - - - - - -

_____

Cut out the letters at the bottom of the page and mix them up. Then paste them in the right squares to finish the sentence:

I like cookies ☐☐☐ milk.

Write the word to finish the sentence:

I like cookies ___ ___ ___ milk.

Write your own sentence using the word:

_____

- - - - - - - - - - - - - - - -

_____

_____

a n d

away

Trace the word and say it aloud:

away   away

The bird is flying **away**.

Write the word:

Cut out the letters at the bottom of the page and mix them up. Then paste them in the right squares to finish the sentence:

The bird is flying [ ][ ][ ][ ] .

Write the word to finish the sentence:

The bird is flying_____.

Write your own sentence using the word:

a w a y

big

Name: _____

Trace the word and say it aloud:

big big big big

An elephant is **big**.

Write the word:

_____

- -

_____

Cut out the letters at the bottom of the page and mix them up. Then paste them in the right squares to finish the sentence:

An elephant is ⬜⬜⬜.

Write the word to finish the sentence:

An elephant is ___ ___ ___.

Write your own sentence using the word:

_____

- -

_____

_____

- -

_____

b i g

blue

Trace the word and say it aloud:

blue blue blue

These jeans are **blue**.

Write the word:

_____

- -

_____

Cut out the letters at the bottom of the page and mix them up. Then paste them in the right squares to finish the sentence:

These jeans are ⬚⬚⬚⬚ .

Write the word to finish the sentence:

These jeans are _____ .

Write your own sentence using the word:

_____

- -

_____

_____

- -

_____

b l u e

can

Name: _____

I **can** ride a bike!

Trace the word and say it aloud: _____

can can can

Write the word:

Cut out the letters at the bottom of the page and mix them up. Then paste them in the right squares to finish the sentence:

I ☐☐☐ ride a bike!

Write the word to finish the sentence:

I ___ ___ ___ ride a bike!

Write your own sentence using the word:

----

c a n

come

Trace the word and say it aloud:

come come

Come here!

Write the word:

Cut out the letters at the bottom of the page and mix them up. Then paste them in the right squares to finish the sentence:

here!

Write the word to finish the sentence:

_____ _____ _____ _____ here!

Write your own sentence using the word:

C o m e

down

Name: _____

Trace the word and say it aloud:

down   down

I'm going **down** the stairs.

Write the word:

_____

- -

_____

Cut out the letters at the bottom of the page and mix them up. Then paste them in the right squares to finish the sentence:

I'm going [ ][ ][ ][ ] the stairs.

Write the word to finish the sentence:

I'm going ___ ___ ___ ___ the stairs.

Write your own sentence using the word:

_____

- -

_____

_____

- -

_____

d o w n

find

Name: _____

Trace the word and say it aloud:

find find find

Let's **find** out
if it flies!

Write the word:

_____

- - - - - - - - - - - - - - - - - - - -

_____

Cut out the letters at the bottom of the page and mix them up. Then paste them in the right squares to finish the sentence:

Let's ☐ ☐ ☐ ☐ out if it flies!

Write the word to finish the sentence:

Let's ___ ___ ___ ___ out if it flies!

Write your own sentence using the word:

_____

- - - - - - - - - - - - - - - - - - - -

_____

- - - - - - - - - - - - - - - - - - - -

_____

f i n d

for

Name: _____

Trace the word and say it aloud:

for   for   for

*It's **for** you!*

Write the word:

_____

- -

_____

Cut out the letters at the bottom of the page and mix them up. Then paste them in the right squares to finish the sentence:

It's ☐☐☐ you!

Write the word to finish the sentence:

It's ___ ___ ___ you!

Write your own sentence using the word:

_____

- -

_____

_____

- -

_____

f o r

funny

Trace the word and say it aloud:

funny   funny

What a **funny** joke!

Write the word:

_____

Cut out the letters at the bottom of the page and mix them up. Then paste them in the right squares to finish the sentence:

What a ☐☐☐☐☐ joke!

Write the word to finish the sentence:

What a _____ joke!

Write your own sentence using the word:

_____

_____

_____

f u n n y

go

Name: _____

Trace the word and say it aloud:

go go go go go

Green means **go**.

Write the word:

_____

- -

_____

Cut out the letters at the bottom of the page and mix them up. Then paste them in the right squares to finish the sentence:

Green means □□.

Write the word to finish the sentence:

Green means ___ ___.

Write your own sentence using the word:

_____

- -

_____

- -

_____

g o

help

Name: _____

Trace the word and say it aloud:

help help help help

Can you **help** me?

Write the word:

_____

- -

_____

Cut out the letters at the bottom of the page and mix them up. Then paste them in the right squares to finish the sentence:

Can you ☐ ☐ ☐ ☐ me?

Write the word to finish the sentence:

Can you _____ me?

Write your own sentence using the word:

_____

- -

_____

_____

- -

_____

h e l p

here

Name: _____

Come **here**!

Trace the word and say it aloud:

here here

Write the word:

_____

- - - - - - - - - - - - - - - - - - -

_____

Cut out the letters at the bottom of the page and mix them up. Then paste them in the right squares to finish the sentence:

Come ☐☐☐☐ !

Write the word to finish the sentence:

Come ___ ___ ___ ___ !

Write your own sentence using the word:

_____

- - - - - - - - - - - - - - - - - - -

_____

- - - - - - - - - - - - - - - - - - -

_____

h e r e

I

Name: _____

Trace the word and say it aloud:

I   I   I   I   I   I

I am six years old.

Write the word:

_____

- -

_____

Cut out the letter at the bottom of the page. Then paste it in the square to finish the sentence:

☐ am six years old.

Write the word to finish the sentence:

___ am six years old.

Write your own sentence using the word:

_____

- -

_____

- -

_____

I

in

Trace the word and say it aloud:

in in in in in in in

*The fox is **in** the box.*

Write the word:

_____

- - - - - - - - - - - - - - - - - - - -

_____

Cut out the letters at the bottom of the page and mix them up. Then paste them in the right squares to finish the sentence:

The fox is ▢▢ the box.

Write the word to finish the sentence:

The fox is ___ the box.

Write your own sentence using the word:

_____

- - - - - - - - - - - - - - - - - - - -

_____

_____

- - - - - - - - - - - - - - - - - - - -

_____

i n

is

Name: _____

Trace the word and say it aloud:

is is is is is is is

The dog is happy.

Write the word:

_____

- - - - - - - - - - - - - - - - - - -

_____

Cut out the letters at the bottom of the page and mix them up. Then paste them in the right squares to finish the sentence:

The dog ☐☐ happy.

Write the word to finish the sentence:

The dog ___ ___ happy.

Write your own sentence using the word:

_____

- - - - - - - - - - - - - - - - - - -

_____

- - - - - - - - - - - - - - - - - - -

_____

i s

it

Name: _____

Trace the word and say it aloud:

it   it   it   it   it   it

*I made **it** myself.*

Write the word:

_____

- - - - - - - - - - - - - - - - - - - -

_____

Cut out the letters at the bottom of the page and mix them up. Then paste them in the right squares to finish the sentence:

I made ⬚⬚ myself.

Write the word to finish the sentence:

I made ___ ___ myself.

Write your own sentence using the word:

_____

- - - - - - - - - - - - - - - - - - - -

_____

_____

- - - - - - - - - - - - - - - - - - - -

_____

i   t

jump

Name: _____

Trace the word and say it aloud:

jump   jump

I can **jump** very high.

Write the word:

_____

- -

_____

Cut out the letters at the bottom of the page and mix them up. Then paste them in the right squares to finish the sentence:

I can ☐☐☐☐ very high.

Write the word to finish the sentence:

I can ___ ___ ___ ___ very high.

Write your own sentence using the word:

_____

- -

_____

- -

_____

j u m p

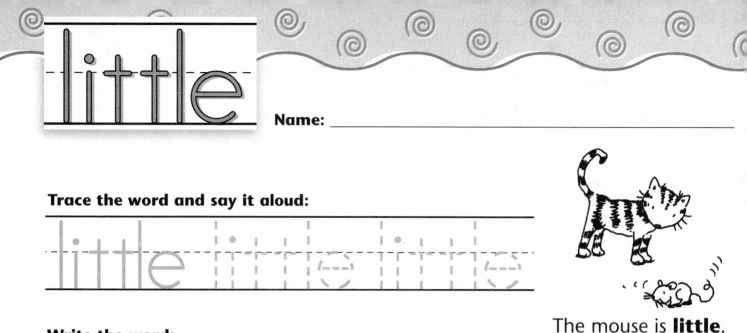

little

Name: _____

Trace the word and say it aloud:

little little little

The mouse is **little**.

Write the word:

_____

- -

_____

Cut out the letters at the bottom of the page and mix them up. Then paste them in the right squares to finish the sentence:

The mouse is ⬚⬚⬚⬚⬚⬚ .

Write the word to finish the sentence:

The mouse is _____ .

Write your own sentence using the word:

_____

- -

_____

_____

- -

_____

✂ l i t t l e

look

Name: _____

Trace the word and say it aloud:

look look look

Look at my new puppy!

Write the word:

_____

- -

_____

Cut out the letters at the bottom of the page and mix them up. Then paste them in the right squares to finish the sentence:

☐ ☐ ☐ ☐ at my new puppy!

Write the word to finish the sentence:

___ ___ ___ ___ at my new puppy!

Write your own sentence using the word:

_____

_____

_____

_____

l o o k

make

Name: _____

Trace the word and say it aloud:

make make

We can **make** a cake!

Write the word:

Cut out the letters at the bottom of the page and mix them up. Then paste them in the right squares to finish the sentence:

We can ☐☐☐☐ a cake!

Write the word to finish the sentence:

We can ___ ___ ___ ___ a cake!

Write your own sentence using the word:

m a k e

me

Name: _____

Trace the word and say it aloud:

me   me   me

This shirt belongs to **me**.

Write the word:

Cut out the letters at the bottom of the page and mix them up. Then paste them in the right squares to finish the sentence:

This shirt belongs to ☐ .

Write the word to finish the sentence:

This shirt belongs to ___ .

Write your own sentence using the word:

m e

my

Name: _____

Trace the word and say it aloud:

my my my

This is **my** cat.

Write the word:

Cut out the letters at the bottom of the page and mix them up. Then paste them in the right squares to finish the sentence:

This is ☐☐ cat.

Write the word to finish the sentence:

This is ___ ___ cat.

Write your own sentence using the word:

m y

not

Name: _____

Trace the word and say it aloud:

not not not

No thanks, I do **not** want any more.

Write the word:

_____

Cut out the letters at the bottom of the page and mix them up. Then paste them in the right squares to finish the sentence:

I do [ ][ ][ ] want any more.

Write the word to finish the sentence:

I do ___ ___ ___ want any more.

Write your own sentence using the word:

_____

_____

_____

n o t

one

Name: _____

Trace the word and say it aloud:

one one one

*I only have **one** shoe.*

Write the word:

_____

Cut out the letters at the bottom of the page and mix them up. Then paste them in the right squares to finish the sentence:

I only have ☐☐☐ shoe.

Write the word to finish the sentence:

I only have ___ ___ ___ shoe.

Write your own sentence using the word:

_____

_____

_____

o n e

play

Name: _____

We **play** soccer.

Trace the word and say it aloud:

play play play

Write the word:

_____

- -

_____

Cut out the letters at the bottom of the page and mix them up. Then paste them in the right squares to finish the sentence:

We ☐☐☐☐ soccer.

Write the word to finish the sentence:

We ___ ___ ___ ___ soccer.

Write your own sentence using the word:

_____

- -

_____

_____

- -

_____

p l a y

red

Name: _____

Trace the word and say it aloud:

red red red

These things are **red**.

Write the word:

_____

- - - - - - - - - - - - - - - -

_____

Cut out the letters at the bottom of the page and mix them up. Then paste them in the right squares to finish the sentence:

These things are ☐☐☐ .

Write the word to finish the sentence:

These things are ____ ____ ____ .

Write your own sentence using the word:

_____

- - - - - - - - - - - - - - - -

_____

- - - - - - - - - - - - - - - -

_____

r e d

run

Name: _____

Trace the word and say it aloud:

run   run   run

*I can **run** fast!*

Write the word:

_____

- - - - - - - - - - - - - - - - - - - -

_____

Cut out the letters at the bottom of the page and mix them up. Then paste them in the right squares to finish the sentence:

I can [ ][ ][ ] fast!

Write the word to finish the sentence:

I can ___ ___ ___ fast!

Write your own sentence using the word:

_____

- - - - - - - - - - - - - - - - - - - -

_____

- - - - - - - - - - - - - - - - - - - -

_____

r u n

said

Name: _____

Mom **said** I could go in the pool.

Trace the word and say it aloud:

said said said

Write the word:

_____

- - - - - - - - - - - - - - - - - - -

_____

Cut out the letters at the bottom of the page and mix them up. Then paste them in the right squares to finish the sentence:

Mom ☐☐☐☐ I could.

Write the word to finish the sentence:

Mom ___ ___ ___ ___ I could.

Write your own sentence using the word:

_____

- - - - - - - - - - - - - - - - - - -

_____

_____

- - - - - - - - - - - - - - - - - - -

_____

s a i d

see

Name: _____

Trace the word and say it aloud:

see   see   see

My glasses help me **see**.

Write the word:

_____

Cut out the letters at the bottom of the page and mix them up. Then paste them in the right squares to finish the sentence:

My glasses help me ☐ ☐ ☐ .

Write the word to finish the sentence:

My glasses help me ___ ___ ___ .

Write your own sentence using the word:

_____

_____

s | e | e

the

Name: _____

Trace the word and say it aloud:

the   the   the

The sun is in the sky.

Write the word:

_____

- - - - - - - - - - - - - - - - - - - -

_____

Cut out the letters at the bottom of the page and mix them up. Then paste them in the right squares to finish the sentence:

☐ ☐ ☐   sun is in the sky.

Write the word to finish the sentence:

___ ___ ___   sun is in the sky.

Write your own sentence using the word:

_____

- - - - - - - - - - - - - - - - - - - -

_____

_____

- - - - - - - - - - - - - - - - - - - -

_____

T h e

three

Name: _____

Trace the word and say it aloud:

three three

I have **three** flowers.

Write the word:

_____

- - - - - - - - - - - - - - - - - - - -

_____

Cut out the letters at the bottom of the page and mix them up. Then paste them in the right squares to finish the sentence:

I have ☐ ☐ ☐ ☐ ☐ flowers.

Write the word to finish the sentence:

I have ___ ___ ___ ___ ___ flowers.

Write your own sentence using the word:

_____

- - - - - - - - - - - - - - - - - - - -

_____

- - - - - - - - - - - - - - - - - - - -

_____

t h r e e

to

Trace the word and say it aloud:

to to to to to

*It's time **to** wake up!*

Write the word:

Cut out the letters at the bottom of the page and mix them up. Then paste them in the right squares to finish the sentence:

It's time ☐☐ wake up!

Write the word to finish the sentence:

It's time ___ wake up!

Write your own sentence using the word:

t   o

two

Name: _____

Trace the word and say it aloud:

two   two   two

*I have **two** eyes.*

Write the word:

_____

- - - - - - - - - - - - - - - - - - - -

_____

Cut out the letters at the bottom of the page and mix them up. Then paste them in the right squares to finish the sentence:

I have ☐☐☐ eyes.

Write the word to finish the sentence:

I have _____ eyes.

Write your own sentence using the word:

_____

- - - - - - - - - - - - - - - - - - - -

_____

_____

- - - - - - - - - - - - - - - - - - - -

_____

t | w | o

up

Name: _____

Trace the word and say it aloud:

up up up up up

I'm walking **up** the stairs.

Write the word:

_____

- - - - - - - - - - - - - - - - - -

_____

Cut out the letters at the bottom of the page and mix them up. Then paste them in the right squares to finish the sentence:

I'm walking ☐☐ the stairs.

Write the word to finish the sentence:

I'm walking ___ the stairs.

Write your own sentence using the word:

_____

- - - - - - - - - - - - - - - - - -

_____

_____

- - - - - - - - - - - - - - - - - -

_____

u p

we

Trace the word and say it aloud:

we we we we

We are on the
same team.

Write the word:

_____

- - - - - - - - - - - - - - - - -

_____

Cut out the letters at the bottom of the page and mix them up. Then paste them in the right squares to finish the sentence:

⬜⬜ are on the same team.

Write the word to finish the sentence:

_____ _____ are on the same team.

Write your own sentence using the word:

_____

- - - - - - - - - - - - - - - - -

_____

_____

- - - - - - - - - - - - - - - - -

_____

We

where

Name: _____

A map tells **where** things are.

Trace the word and say it aloud:

where where

Write the word:

_____

- - - - - - - - - - - - - - - -

_____

Cut out the letters at the bottom of the page and mix them up. Then paste them in the right squares to finish the sentence:

A map tells ☐ ☐ ☐ ☐ ☐ things are.

Write the word to finish the sentence:

A map tells _____ things are.

Write your own sentence using the word:

_____

- - - - - - - - - - - - - - - -

_____

_____

- - - - - - - - - - - - - - - -

_____

w h e r e

yellow

These things are **yellow**.

Trace the word and say it aloud:

yellow yellow

Write the word:

Cut out the letters at the bottom of the page and mix them up. Then paste them in the right squares to finish the sentence:

These things are ⬚⬚⬚⬚⬚⬚.

Write the word to finish the sentence:

These things are _____.

Write your own sentence using the word:

y e l l o w

you

Name: _____

Trace the word and say it aloud: _____

you   you   you

Hello, how are **you**?

Write the word:

_____

- -

_____

Cut out the letters at the bottom of the page and mix them up. Then paste them in the right squares to finish the sentence:

Hello, how are ☐☐☐ ?

Write the word to finish the sentence:

Hello, how are _____ ?

Write your own sentence using the word:

_____

- -

_____

- -

_____

y o u

all

I have **all** the crayons!

Trace the word and say it aloud:

all all all all all

Write the word:

_____

- - - - - - - - - - - - - - - - - - -

_____

Cut out the letters at the bottom of the page and mix them up. Then paste them in the right squares to finish the sentence:

I have ☐☐☐ the crayons!

Write the word to finish the sentence:

I have ___ ___ ___ the crayons!

Write your own sentence using the word:

_____

- - - - - - - - - - - - - - - - - - -

_____

_____

a l l

am

Name: _____

Trace the word and say it aloud: _____

am am am am

*I **am** very tall.*

Write the word:

- -

Cut out the letters at the bottom of the page and mix them up. Then paste them in the right squares to finish the sentence:

I ☐☐ very tall.

Write the word to finish the sentence:

I ____ ____ very tall.

Write your own sentence using the word:

- -

- -

a m

are

Name: _____

Trace the word and say it aloud:

are   are   are

*Hello, how **are** you?*

Write the word:

Cut out the letters at the bottom of the page and mix them up. Then paste them in the right squares to finish the sentence:

Hello, how ▢▢▢ you?

Write the word to finish the sentence:

Hello, how ____ ____ ____ you?

Write your own sentence using the word:

a   r   e

at

Name: _____

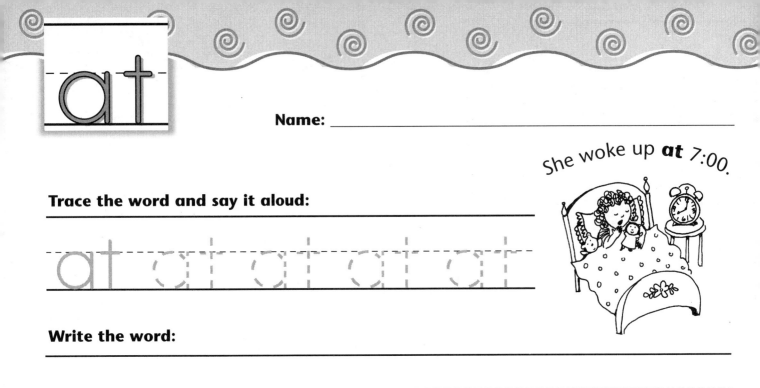

She woke up **at** 7:00.

Trace the word and say it aloud:

at at at at at at

Write the word:

Cut out the letters at the bottom of the page and mix them up. Then paste them in the right squares to finish the sentence:

She woke up ☐☐ 7:00.

Write the word to finish the sentence:

She woke up ___ 7:00.

Write your own sentence using the word:

a t

ate

Name: _____

Trace the word and say it aloud:

ate   ate   ate

*I **ate** a lot of cake.*

Write the word:

Cut out the letters at the bottom of the page and mix them up. Then paste them in the right squares to finish the sentence:

I ☐☐☐ a lot of cake.

Write the word to finish the sentence:

I _____ a lot of cake.

Write your own sentence using the word:

a   t   e

be

Name: _____

Trace the word and say it aloud:

be be be be

When I grow up,
I want to **be** a doctor.

Write the word:

_____

- - - - - - - - - - - - - - - - - - - -

_____

Cut out the letters at the bottom of the page and mix them up. Then paste them in the right squares to finish the sentence:

I want to ☐☐ a doctor.

Write the word to finish the sentence:

I want to ___ ___ a doctor.

Write your own sentence using the word:

_____

- - - - - - - - - - - - - - - - - - - -

_____

_____

- - - - - - - - - - - - - - - - - - - -

_____

b e

black

Name: _____

Trace the word and say it aloud:

black black

At night, the sky is usually **black**.

Write the word:

_____

- - - - - - - - - - - - - - - - - - - -

_____

Cut out the letters at the bottom of the page and mix them up. Then paste them in the right squares to finish the sentence:

The sky is usually ☐☐☐☐☐.

Write the word to finish the sentence:

The sky is usually _____.

Write your own sentence using the word:

_____

_____

_____

b l a c k

brown

Name: _____

Trace the word and say it aloud:

brown brown

This is a **brown** bear.

Write the word:

_____

- - - - - - - - - - - - - - - - -

_____

Cut out the letters at the bottom of the page and mix them up. Then paste them in the right squares to finish the sentence:

This is a ☐☐☐☐☐ bear.

Write the word to finish the sentence:

This is a _____ bear.

Write your own sentence using the word:

_____

- - - - - - - - - - - - - - - - -

_____

- - - - - - - - - - - - - - - - -

_____

b r o w n

but

Name: _____

Trace the word and say it aloud:

but but but

A mouse is small,
but *a fly is smaller.*

Write the word:

_____

- - - - - - - - - - - - - - - - - - - -

_____

Cut out the letters at the bottom of the page and mix them up. Then paste them in the right squares to finish the sentence:

A mouse is small, [   ] a fly is smaller.

Write the word to finish the sentence:

A mouse is small, _____ a fly is smaller.

Write your own sentence using the word:

_____

- - - - - - - - - - - - - - - - - - - -

_____

_____

- - - - - - - - - - - - - - - - - - - -

_____

b u t

came

Name: _____

Trace the word and say it aloud:

came came

The bear **came**
out the cave.

Write the word:

Cut out the letters at the bottom of the page and mix them up. Then paste them in the right squares to finish the sentence:

The bear ☐☐☐☐ out.

Write the word to finish the sentence:

The bear ___ ___ ___ ___ out.

Write your own sentence using the word:

c a m e

did

Name: _____

Trace the word and say it aloud:

did did did

I **did** all my
homework.

Write the word:

_____

- - - - - - - - - - - - - - - - - - - -

_____

Cut out the letters at the bottom of the page and mix them up. Then paste them in the right squares to finish the sentence:

I ☐ ☐ ☐ all my homework.

Write the word to finish the sentence:

I ___ ___ ___ all my homework.

Write your own sentence using the word:

_____

- - - - - - - - - - - - - - - - - - - -

_____

- - - - - - - - - - - - - - - - - - - -

_____

d i d

eat

Name: _____

Trace the word and say it aloud:

eat eat eat

What should I **eat**?

Write the word:

Cut out the letters at the bottom of the page and mix them up. Then paste them in the right squares to finish the sentence:

What should I ☐☐☐ ?

Write the word to finish the sentence:

What should I ___ ___ ___ ?

Write your own sentence using the word:

e   a   t

four

Name: _____

Trace the word and say it aloud:

four four four

*I have **four** crayons.*

Write the word:

_____

- - - - - - - - - - - - - - - - - - -

_____

Cut out the letters at the bottom of the page and mix them up. Then paste them in the right squares to finish the sentence:

I have ☐☐☐☐ crayons.

Write the word to finish the sentence:

I have ___ ___ ___ ___ crayons.

Write your own sentence using the word:

_____

- - - - - - - - - - - - - - - - - - -

_____

- - - - - - - - - - - - - - - - - - -

_____

f o u r

get

Name: _____

Trace the word and say it aloud:

get get get

Could you **get** me the truck?

Write the word:

_____

Cut out the letters at the bottom of the page and mix them up. Then paste them in the right squares to finish the sentence:

Could you ☐☐☐ me the truck?

Write the word to finish the sentence:

Could you _____ me the truck?

Write your own sentence using the word:

_____

_____

g e t

good

Name: _____

Trace the word and say it aloud:

good   good

Ice cream tastes good.

Write the word:

_____

Cut out the letters at the bottom of the page and mix them up. Then paste them in the right squares to finish the sentence:

Ice cream tastes [ ][ ][ ][ ] .

Write the word to finish the sentence:

Ice cream tastes _____ .

Write your own sentence using the word:

_____

g o o d

have

Name: _____

Trace the word and say it aloud:

have   have

I **have** a new pet.

Write the word:

Cut out the letters at the bottom of the page and mix them up. Then paste them in the right squares to finish the sentence:

I ☐☐☐☐ a new pet.

Write the word to finish the sentence:

I _____ a new pet.

Write your own sentence using the word:

h a v e

into

He dove **into** the pool.

Trace the word and say it aloud:

into into into

Write the word:

Cut out the letters at the bottom of the page and mix them up. Then paste them in the right squares to finish the sentence:

He dove ☐☐☐☐ the pool.

Write the word to finish the sentence:

He dove ___ ___ ___ ___ the pool.

Write your own sentence using the word:

into

i n t o

like

Name: _____

I **like** to swim.

Trace the word and say it aloud:

like   like   like

Write the word:

_____

- -

_____

Cut out the letters at the bottom of the page and mix them up. Then paste them in the right squares to finish the sentence:

I ☐☐☐☐ to swim.

Write the word to finish the sentence:

I ___ ___ ___ ___ to swim.

Write your own sentence using the word:

_____

- -

_____

- -

_____

l i k e

must

Name: _____

Trace the word and say it aloud:

must   must

That **must** be yummy.

Write the word:

_____

- - - - - - - - - - - - - - - - - -

_____

Cut out the letters at the bottom of the page and mix them up. Then paste them in the right squares to finish the sentence:

That ☐ ☐ ☐ ☐ be yummy.

Write the word to finish the sentence:

That ___ ___ ___ ___ be yummy.

Write your own sentence using the word:

_____

- - - - - - - - - - - - - - - - - -

_____

_____

- - - - - - - - - - - - - - - - - -

_____

m u s t

new

Name: _____

Trace the word and say it aloud:

new new new

*I have **new** shoes.*

Write the word:

_____

- - - - - - - - - - - - - - - - - - -

_____

Cut out the letters at the bottom of the page and mix them up. Then paste them in the right squares to finish the sentence:

I have ⬚⬚⬚ shoes.

Write the word to finish the sentence:

I have ___ ___ ___ shoes.

Write your own sentence using the word:

_____

- - - - - - - - - - - - - - - - - - -

_____

_____

- - - - - - - - - - - - - - - - - - -

_____

n e w

no

Name: _____

Trace the word and say it aloud:

no no no no no no

No thanks, I'm full.

Write the word:

- -

Cut out the letters at the bottom of the page and mix them up. Then paste them in the right squares to finish the sentence:

☐ ☐ thanks, I'm full.

Write the word to finish the sentence:

____ ____ thanks, I'm full.

Write your own sentence using the word:

- -

- -

N o

now

Name: _____

Trace the word and say it aloud:

now now now

We have to leave **now**.

Write the word:

- -

Cut out the letters at the bottom of the page and mix them up. Then paste them in the right squares to finish the sentence:

We have to leave ☐☐☐.

Write the word to finish the sentence:

We have to leave ___ ___ ___.

Write your own sentence using the word:

- -

- -

n o w

on

Trace the word and say it aloud:

on on on on on on

Dinner is **on** the table.

Write the word:

Cut out the letters at the bottom of the page and mix them up. Then paste them in the right squares to finish the sentence:

Dinner is ⬚⬚ the table.

Write the word to finish the sentence:

Dinner is ___ ___ the table.

Write your own sentence using the word:

o n

our

Name: _____

Trace the word and say it aloud:

our　　our　　our

This is my family, and this is **our** house.

Write the word:

Cut out the letters at the bottom of the page and mix them up. Then paste them in the right squares to finish the sentence:

This is ⬚⬚⬚ house.

Write the word to finish the sentence:

This is ___ ___ ___ house.

Write your own sentence using the word:

o u r

out

Name: _____

The hat is **out**
of the box.

Trace the word and say it aloud:

out   out   out

Write the word:

_____

- - - - - - - - - - - - - - - - - - - -

_____

Cut out the letters at the bottom of the page and mix them up. Then paste them in the right squares to finish the sentence:

The hat is ☐☐☐ of the box.

Write the word to finish the sentence:

The hat is ___ ___ ___ of the box.

Write your own sentence using the word:

_____

- - - - - - - - - - - - - - - - - - - -

_____

- - - - - - - - - - - - - - - - - - - -

_____

o u t

please

Name: _____

May I speak to
Joey, **please**?

Trace the word and say it aloud:

please please

Write the word:

_____

- -

_____

Cut out the letters at the bottom of the page and mix them up. Then paste them in the right squares to finish the sentence:

May I speak to Joey, ☐☐☐☐☐☐ ?

Write the word to finish the sentence:

May I speak to Joey, _____ ?

Write your own sentence using the word:

_____

- -

_____

_____

- -

_____

p l e a s e

pretty

Name: _____

What a **pretty** butterfly!

Trace the word and say it aloud:

pretty pretty

Write the word:

_____

- -

_____

Cut out the letters at the bottom of the page and mix them up. Then paste them in the right squares to finish the sentence:

What a ☐☐☐☐☐☐ butterfly!

Write the word to finish the sentence:

What a _____ butterfly!

Write your own sentence using the word:

_____

- -

_____

- -

_____

p r e t t y

ran

Trace the word and say it aloud:

ran ran ran

*I just **ran** in a race.*

Write the word:

Cut out the letters at the bottom of the page and mix them up. Then paste them in the right squares to finish the sentence:

I just ⬚⬚⬚ in a race.

Write the word to finish the sentence:

I just _____ in a race.

Write your own sentence using the word:

r a n

ride

Name: _____

I can **ride** a horse.

Trace the word and say it aloud:

ride ride ride

Write the word:

_____

- - - - - - - - - - - - - - - -

_____

Cut out the letters at the bottom of the page and mix them up. Then paste them in the right squares to finish the sentence:

I can ☐☐☐☐ a horse.

Write the word to finish the sentence:

I can ___ ___ ___ ___ a horse.

Write your own sentence using the word:

_____

- - - - - - - - - - - - - - - -

_____

_____

- - - - - - - - - - - - - - - -

_____

r i d e

saw

Name: _____

Trace the word and say it aloud:

saw saw saw

I **saw** mountains on my vacation.

Write the word:

Cut out the letters at the bottom of the page and mix them up. Then paste them in the right squares to finish the sentence:

I ☐☐☐ mountains.

Write the word to finish the sentence:

I ___ ___ ___ mountains.

Write your own sentence using the word:

s a w

say

Name: _____

It is time to **say** goodnight.

Trace the word and say it aloud:

say   say   say

Write the word:

_____

- - - - - - - - - - - - - - - - - - - -

_____

Cut out the letters at the bottom of the page and mix them up. Then paste them in the right squares to finish the sentence:

It is time to ☐☐☐ goodnight.

Write the word to finish the sentence:

It is time to _____ goodnight.

Write your own sentence using the word:

_____

- - - - - - - - - - - - - - - - - - - -

_____

_____

- - - - - - - - - - - - - - - - - - - -

_____

s a y

she

Name: _____

Trace the word and say it aloud:

she   she   she

This is Jen, **she** is
my best friend.

Write the word:

_____

- -

_____

Cut out the letters at the bottom of the page and mix them up. Then paste them in the right squares to finish the sentence:

☐ ☐ ☐ is my best friend.

Write the word to finish the sentence:

_____ _____ _____ is my best friend.

Write your own sentence using the word:

_____

- -

_____

- -

_____

S h e

SO

Name: _____

Trace the word and say it aloud:

SO   SO   SO   SO

Wow! Dinosaurs
were **so** big!

Write the word:

- -

_____

Cut out the letters at the bottom of the page and mix them up. Then paste them in the right squares to finish the sentence:

Dinosaurs were ⬚⬚ big!

Write the word to finish the sentence:

Dinosaurs were ___ big!

Write your own sentence using the word:

- -

_____

- -

_____

S   O

soon

Name: _____

Trace the word and say it aloud:

soon soon

Soon it will be 9:00.

Write the word:

Cut out the letters at the bottom of the page and mix them up. Then paste them in the right squares to finish the sentence:

| | | | | it will be 9:00.

Write the word to finish the sentence:

_____ _____ _____ _____ it will be 9:00.

Write your own sentence using the word:

S o o n

that

Name: _____

Trace the word and say it aloud:

that that that

That was a delicious pizza.

Write the word:

_____

- -

_____

Cut out the letters at the bottom of the page and mix them up. Then paste them in the right squares to finish the sentence:

[ ] [ ] [ ] [ ] was a delicious pizza.

Write the word to finish the sentence:

___ ___ ___ ___ was a delicious pizza.

Write your own sentence using the word:

_____

- -

_____

_____

- -

_____

T h a t

there

Name: _____

Trace the word and say it aloud:

there   there

My dog is over **there**.

Write the word:

_____

- - - - - - - - - - - - - - -

_____

Cut out the letters at the bottom of the page and mix them up. Then paste them in the right squares to finish the sentence:

My dog is over ⬚⬚⬚⬚⬚ .

Write the word to finish the sentence:

My dog is over _____ .

Write your own sentence using the word:

_____

- - - - - - - - - - - - - - -

_____

- - - - - - - - - - - - - - -

_____

t h e r e

they

Name: _____

Trace the word and say it aloud:

they   they

Meet Jen and Jan.
They are twins.

Write the word:

_____

- -

_____

Cut out the letters at the bottom of the page and mix them up. Then paste them in the right squares to finish the sentence:

are twins.

Write the word to finish the sentence:

____ ____ ____ ____ are twins.

Write your own sentence using the word:

_____

- -

_____

_____

- -

_____

T h e y

this

Name: _____

Trace the word and say it aloud:

this this this

This is Matt and Dan.
They are twins.

Write the word:

_____

- -

_____

Cut out the letters at the bottom of the page and mix them up. Then paste them in the right squares to finish the sentence:

☐ ☐ ☐ ☐ is Matt and Dan.

Write the word to finish the sentence:

____ ____ ____ ____ is Matt and Dan.

Write your own sentence using the word:

_____

- -

_____

- -

_____

| T | h | i | s |

too

Name: _____

This shirt is **too** big.

Trace the word and say it aloud:

too   too   too

Write the word:

_____

_ _ _ _ _ _ _ _ _ _ _ _ _ _ _ _

_____

Cut out the letters at the bottom of the page and mix them up. Then paste them in the right squares to finish the sentence:

This shirt is ▢▢ big.

Write the word to finish the sentence:

This shirt is ____ big.

Write your own sentence using the word:

_____

_ _ _ _ _ _ _ _ _ _ _ _ _ _ _ _

_____

_____

_ _ _ _ _ _ _ _ _ _ _ _ _ _ _ _

_____

t   o   o

under

Name: _____

The cat is **under** the table.

Trace the word and say it aloud:

under   under

Write the word:

Cut out the letters at the bottom of the page and mix them up. Then paste them in the right squares to finish the sentence:

The cat is ⬜⬜⬜⬜⬜ the table.

Write the word to finish the sentence:

The cat is _____ the table.

Write your own sentence using the word:

u n d e r

want

Trace the word and say it aloud:

want   want

Do you **want** some more?

Write the word:

_____

- -

_____

Cut out the letters at the bottom of the page and mix them up. Then paste them in the right squares to finish the sentence:

Do you ☐☐☐☐ some more?

Write the word to finish the sentence:

Do you ___ ___ ___ ___ some more?

Write your own sentence using the word:

_____

- -

_____

_____

- -

_____

w a n t

was

Name: _____

Trace the word and say it aloud:
_____

was   was   was

This is me when
*I **was** a baby.*

Write the word:
_____

- -

_____

Cut out the letters at the bottom of the page and mix them up. Then paste them in the right squares to finish the sentence:

This is me when I ☐☐☐ a baby.

Write the word to finish the sentence:

This is me when I ____ a baby.

Write your own sentence using the word:
_____

- -

_____

- -

_____

w   a   s

well

Name: _____

Trace the word and say it aloud:

well well well

I play the piano **well.**

Write the word:

_____

- - - - - - - - - - - - - - - - - - - -

_____

Cut out the letters at the bottom of the page and mix them up. Then paste them in the right squares to finish the sentence:

I play the piano ⬜⬜⬜⬜.

Write the word to finish the sentence:

I play the piano _____.

Write your own sentence using the word:

_____

- - - - - - - - - - - - - - - - - - - -

_____

- - - - - - - - - - - - - - - - - - - -

_____

w e l l

went

Name: _____

Trace the word and say it aloud:

went   went

Yesterday I **went**
to the park.

Write the word:

Cut out the letters at the bottom of the page and mix them up. Then paste them in the right squares to finish the sentence:

I ☐☐☐☐ to the park.

Write the word to finish the sentence:

I ___ ___ ___ ___ to the park.

Write your own sentence using the word:

w e n t

what

Name: _____

What time is it?

Trace the word and say it aloud:

what ~~what~~

Write the word:

_____

- -

_____

Cut out the letters at the bottom of the page and mix them up. Then paste them in the right squares to finish the sentence:

☐ ☐ ☐ ☐   time is it?

Write the word to finish the sentence:

____ ____ ____ ____   time is it?

Write your own sentence using the word:

_____

- -

_____

_____

- -

_____

W h a t

white

Name: _____

Trace the word and say it aloud:

white   white

These things are **white**.

Write the word:

_____

- -

_____

Cut out the letters at the bottom of the page and mix them up. Then paste them in the right squares to finish the sentence:

These things are ▢▢▢▢▢.

Write the word to finish the sentence:

These things are ___ ___ ___ ___ ___.

Write your own sentence using the word:

_____

- -

_____

- -

_____

w h i t e

who

Name: _____

Trace the word and say it aloud:

who   who   who

Write the word:

_____

- -

_____

Cut out the letters at the bottom of the page and mix them up. Then paste them in the right squares to finish the sentence:

wants to play?

Write the word to finish the sentence:

____ ____ ____ wants to play?

Write your own sentence using the word:

_____

- -

_____

_____

- -

_____

W h o

will

Name: _____

Trace the word and say it aloud:

will   will   will

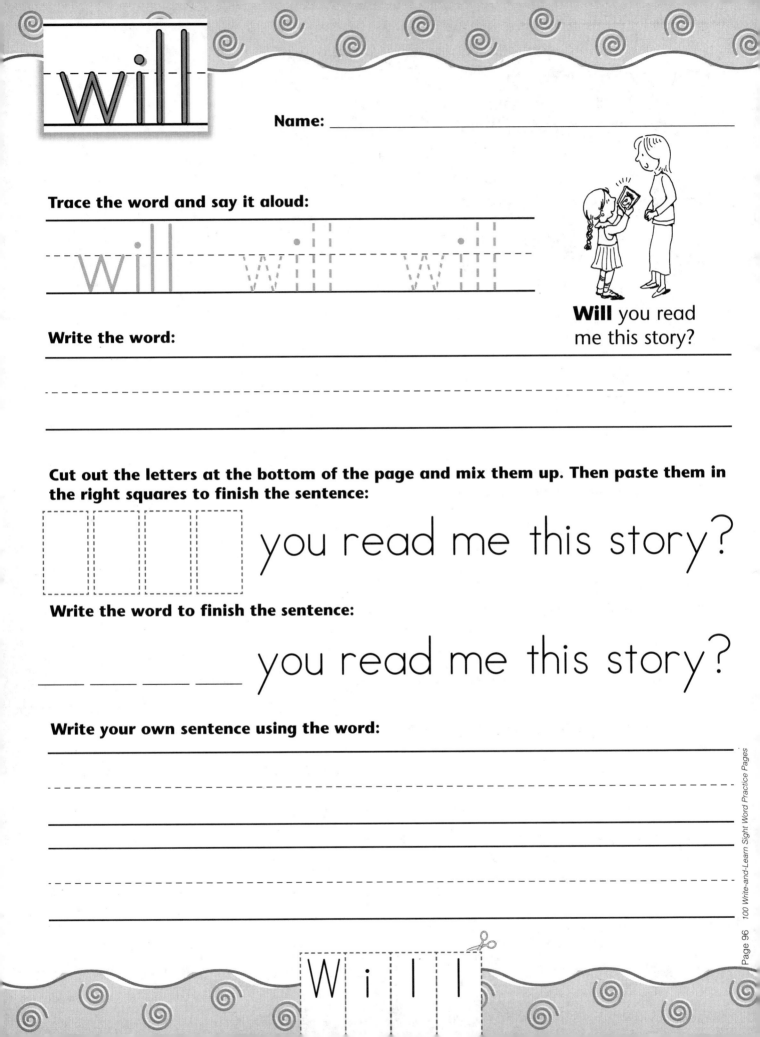

Will you read me this story?

Write the word:

_____

- - - - - - - - - - - - - - - - - - -

_____

Cut out the letters at the bottom of the page and mix them up. Then paste them in the right squares to finish the sentence:

☐☐☐☐ you read me this story?

Write the word to finish the sentence:

___ ___ ___ ___ you read me this story?

Write your own sentence using the word:

_____

- - - - - - - - - - - - - - - - - - -

_____

- - - - - - - - - - - - - - - - - - -

_____

W i l l

with

Name: _____

Trace the word and say it aloud:

with with with

I want a burger **with** *fries.*

Write the word:

_____

- - - - - - - - - - - - - - - - - - -

_____

Cut out the letters at the bottom of the page and mix them up. Then paste them in the right squares to finish the sentence:

I want a burger ☐☐☐☐ fries.

Write the word to finish the sentence:

I want a burger _____ fries.

Write your own sentence using the word:

_____

- - - - - - - - - - - - - - - - - - -

_____

- - - - - - - - - - - - - - - - - - -

_____

w i t h

yes

Name: _____

Trace the word and say it aloud:

yes   yes   yes

Yes, please!

Write the word:

_____

- -

_____

Cut out the letters at the bottom of the page and mix them up. Then paste them in the right squares to finish the sentence:

☐ ☐ ☐ , please!

Write the word to finish the sentence:

_____ _____ _____ , please!

Write your own sentence using the word:

_____

- -

_____

_____

- -

_____

Y e s

after

Name: _____

Trace the word and say it aloud:

after   after

After my socks,
I put on my shoes.

Write the word:

_____

Cut out the letters at the bottom of the page and mix them up. Then paste them in the right squares to finish the sentence:

[ ][ ][ ][ ] my socks, I put on shoes.

Write the word to finish the sentence:

_____ my socks, I put on shoes.

Write your own sentence using the word:

_____

_____

_____

A f t e r

again

That was fun. Lets play **again**!

Trace the word and say it aloud:

again again

Write the word:

_____

- - - - - - - - - - - - - - - - - - - -

_____

Cut out the letters at the bottom of the page and mix them up. Then paste them in the right squares to finish the sentence:

Let's play ☐☐☐☐☐ !

Write the word to finish the sentence:

Let's play _____ !

Write your own sentence using the word:

_____

- - - - - - - - - - - - - - - - - - - -

_____

_____

- - - - - - - - - - - - - - - - - - - -

_____

a g a i n

an

Name: _____

Trace the word and say it aloud:

an   an   an   an

An elephant is big!

Write the word:

_____

- -

_____

Cut out the letters at the bottom of the page and mix them up. Then paste them in the right squares to finish the sentence:

☐☐ elephant is big!

Write the word to finish the sentence:

___ ___ elephant is big!

Write your own sentence using the word:

_____

- -

_____

- -

_____

A n

any

Name: _____

Trace the word and say it aloud:

any   any   any

*Are there **any** birds in the tree?*

Write the word:

_____

- -

_____

Cut out the letters at the bottom of the page and mix them up. Then paste them in the right squares to finish the sentence:

Are there ☐☐☐ birds?

Write the word to finish the sentence:

Are there ___ ___ ___ birds?

Write your own sentence using the word:

_____

- -

_____

_____

- -

_____

a n y

as

Trace the word and say it aloud:

as   as   as   as

The kitten is
white **as** snow.

Write the word:

Cut out the letters at the bottom of the page and mix them up. Then paste them in the right squares to finish the sentence:

The kitten is white ⬚⬚ snow.

Write the word to finish the sentence:

The kitten is white ____ snow.

Write your own sentence using the word:

a s

ask

Name: _____

Trace the word and say it aloud:

ask   ask   ask

*May I **ask** a question?*

Write the word:

_____

- -

_____

Cut out the letters at the bottom of the page and mix them up. Then paste them in the right squares to finish the sentence:

May I ⬚⬚⬚ a question?

Write the word to finish the sentence:

May I ___ ___ ___ a question?

Write your own sentence using the word:

_____

- -

_____

- -

_____

a s k

by

Name: _____

Trace the word and say it aloud:

by by by by

This book is **by** my favorite author.

Write the word:

_____

- - - - - - - - - - - - - - - - - - -

_____

Cut out the letters at the bottom of the page and mix them up. Then paste them in the right squares to finish the sentence:

This book is ☐☐ my favorite author.

Write the word to finish the sentence:

This book is ____ my favorite author.

Write your own sentence using the word:

_____

- - - - - - - - - - - - - - - - - - -

_____

- - - - - - - - - - - - - - - - - - -

_____

b y

could

Name: _____

Trace the word and say it aloud:

could   could

I wanted to see if it **could** float. It can!

Write the word:

_____

- -

_____

Cut out the letters at the bottom of the page and mix them up. Then paste them in the right squares to finish the sentence:

I wanted to see if it ☐☐☐☐☐ float.

Write the word to finish the sentence:

I wanted to see if it _____ float.

Write your own sentence using the word:

_____

- -

_____

- -

_____

c o u l d

every

Name: _____

Trace the word and say it aloud:

every every

I brush my teeth
every *day.*

Write the word:

_____

- - - - - - - - - - - - - - - - - - - -

_____

Cut out the letters at the bottom of the page and mix them up. Then paste them in the right squares to finish the sentence:

I brush my teeth ☐☐☐☐ day.

Write the word to finish the sentence:

I brush my teeth _____ day.

Write your own sentence using the word:

_____

- - - - - - - - - - - - - - - - - - - -

_____

_____

- - - - - - - - - - - - - - - - - - - -

_____

e v e r y

fly

These things can **fly**.

Trace the word and say it aloud:

fly fly fly fly

Write the word:

_____

- -

_____

Cut out the letters at the bottom of the page and mix them up. Then paste them in the right squares to finish the sentence:

These things can ☐☐☐.

Write the word to finish the sentence:

These things can ___ ___ ___.

Write your own sentence using the word:

_____

- -

_____

_____

- -

_____

f l y

Word Search

a	n	b	e	b	i	g	f	o	r
n	a	l	o	i	s	v	u	n	m
d	p	u	g	g	o	t	n	m	a
w	q	e	b	c	n	h	l	k	k
e	r	d	c	h	e	r	j	s	e
c	f	e	i	i	h	e	i	e	u
r	u	n	t	u	p	e	s	e	t
d	o	w	n	a	m	a	k	o	n
l	w	e	r	t	o	p	m	y	t
y	o	u	m	p	l	a	y	a	m

How many words can you find? Circle them and write them on the lines.

up	her	an	it
go	a	am	be
you	i	set	an
play	he	sic	my
down	for	make	is

Word Search

t	l	r	q	p	c	d	i	d	a
h	h	i	j	k	a	y	m	n	e
e	a	t	f	g	m	z	o	f	v
r	s	h	a	v	e	d	u	o	v
e	t	e	e	d	c	c	n	u	w
u	p	y	e	s	b	a	d	r	g
v	l	b	w	o	u	t	e	d	v
w	e	x	h	o	y	z	r	i	h
r	a	q	i	n	o	w	b	n	i
o	s	p	t	c	u	k	j	t	u
n	e	m	e	l	r	s	t	o	a

How many words can you find? Circle them and write them on the lines.

_____ _____ _____ _____

_____ _____ _____ _____

_____ _____ _____ _____

_____ _____ _____ _____

Sight Word Bingo

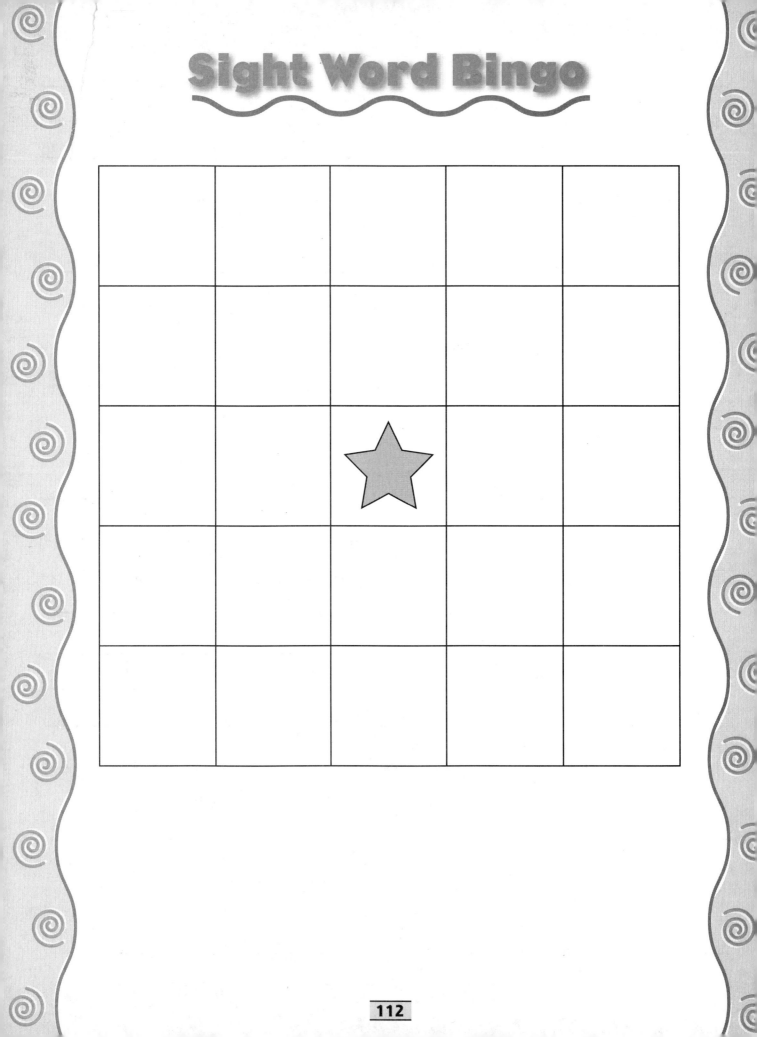